ALL THE STEPS
I HAVE TAKEN

ALL THE STEPS I HAVE TAKEN

THEN AND NOW

LINDA L. CHRISTIANSON

InspiringVoices®
A Service of **Guideposts**

Inspiring Voices books may be ordered through booksellers or by contacting:

Inspiring Voices
1663 Liberty Drive
Bloomington, IN 47403
www.inspiringvoices.com
1-(866) 697-5313

ISBN: 978-1-4624-0234-2 (sc)
ISBN: 978-1-4624-0233-5 (e)

Library of Congress Control Number: 2012912268

Printed in the United States of America

Inspiring Voices rev. date: 08/03/2012

Dedicated to my family:

Nolan

Tonya

Bob

Aaron

Jessie

Lianna

Travis

Cody

Emma

Ryan

Cole

Anika

Cade

Addison

Aden

Their support has always been there for me.

Contents

Preface

We all have adjustments and situations that we must live with. This narrative describes the adjustments that shaped the person I am today.

As an infant, six months old, I was diagnosed with poliomyelitis, a highly contagious disease that crippled thousands of children and adults before a vaccine became available in 1953. My parents never stopped me from attempting challenges that came my way, and I will always be grateful to them. I am very appreciative of my wonderful husband for choosing me with my limitation. We have journeyed together for forty-three wonderful years. My life has been a voyage that has given me a magnificent family, superlative set of friends with whom I share my life, and a home I can be devoted to and care for. I have become committed to my small rural country church, Red Oak Grove Lutheran Church, near Austin, Minnesota. This church family has nurtured and prayed for me my entire life. I am grateful for a forty-two-year career as a registered dental assistant. A career that was gratifying and rewarding.

Few people today are aware of polio. They may never cross paths with someone who has had it, someone who has been forced to spend his or her life trying to be as normal as possible and build a life worth living. Polio made me a very determined and strong-willed person, and I will share with you the journey that gave me much happiness and success.

At this time of the morning, I'm not sure what the day has in store for me. It is still dark outside, and I hear no wind, so perhaps no storm is brewing. I'll just have to wait and see. The crutches are there against the bedroom wall, just where I put them last evening as I went to bed. It hasn't always been this way. I still remember the days when I could get along as a more normal person, but that is changing more quickly than I'd like to admit. It makes me appreciate what I can do and continue to do each day of my life. One of the things polio sufferers were taught early on was to be as normal as possible. For many that was a difficult task. For me contracting polio at such a young age made it easier to be normal, because the way I was seemed normal to me. I never knew any other way of getting around. The crutches get me to the laundry room to sort and start the laundry, and then to the kitchen to start the coffee. After I've read my Thomas Kinkade devotional reading for the day, I am ready to move forward and make my day the best it can be.

I'll start *All the Steps I Have Taken* with a quotation from *Guidepost*, a wonderful magazine my mother-in-law introduced me to when my husband and I were married. She had been enjoying the magazine for many years and gave me my first subscription. I have continued to get pleasure from and share all the finished magazines with friends. The quotation from a Guidepost magazine column "The Up Side of Today's Positive Thinkers": "God rarely makes our fears disappear. Instead, he asks us to be strong and take courage. Courage is not the absence of fear. You could say that without fear, you can't have genuine courage." I have faced many situations in my lifetime that have led me to experience fear, and these have helped me to be more courageous.

The medical name for the disease is anterior poliomyelitis or infantile paralysis. It is a disease caused by a virus that can be either inhaled or swallowed. Polio may seem at first like a number of other diseases that start with a fever, headache, fatigue, and sore throat. In many cases, the disease never goes beyond these first symptoms. Sometimes it continues, and certain muscles become weak; eventually, the virus reaches the brain and spinal cord, destroying the anterior horn cells of the central nervous system and thus paralyzing the muscles. Sometimes patients were paralyzed to the extent that they could breathe only with the help of a mechanical ventilator or "iron lung." I was fortunate; the only connection I had to an iron lung was that I saw them in hospital rooms and felt so sorry for the patients who were in them.

Poliomyelitis is derived from two Greek words: *polios*, meaning, "gray" and *myelos*, meaning, "matter." These words refer to specific parts of the brain and spinal cord: nerve cells that send impulses to muscle cells. These cells have a darker appearance than other parts of the nervous system, appearing gray in color. These cells are clustered in the front half of the spinal cord and that is where the name anterior poliomyelitis comes from. A virus is a small organism or living thing that multiplies when inside a living cell. It is the virus that is able to infect and damage these nerve cells, causing them to not activate the muscle cells. Weakness or paralysis is the end result. Polio usually afflicts children and was once one of the most feared diseases. Polio is not new. Polio deformities were drawn on cave walls in the Middle Ages, portraying the weakness the disease caused.

Since three different kinds of poliovirus exist, a vaccine was needed that would protect against all three strains. In 1953, a vaccine developed by Dr. Jonas Salk and his colleagues at the University of Pittsburgh became available. Dr. Salk began field trials of his vaccine, which was made from individual strains of poliovirus that had been killed by formalin. This was an injected vaccine, or a shot. It was very effective, and the number of polio cases was reduced drastically. A notable scientist, John Enders, and his team discovered how to grow poliovirus in test tubes a few years before the polio vaccine was discovered. Enders received the Nobel Prize given for polio research in 1954. In 1961, Dr. Albert Sabin, a Russian, developed a second vaccine, which could be taken by mouth. Though living, the ability of the viruses to cause illness had been removed. This vaccine replaced the Salk vaccine and was given in doctors' offices and school lunchrooms across the United States. I remember going to our cafeteria at school in seventh grade and lining up for the oral vaccine. I have asked many, in the medical field, why I would have had to have the vaccine since I already had polio and no one can give me an answer. American courts have addressed many times legal issues of whether government can compel vaccinations and have repeatedly supported immunizations. The Center of Disease Control and Prevention believes that parents should be fully informed of risks and benefits of vaccinations. They give permission before vaccines can be administered. It is a requirement before children can enter school. The number of cases of polio in the United States has dropped steadily since the discovery of the first vaccine, but the disease has not been wiped out. It still exists, and the threat of infection is always there in our country and others.

Lifeline and Headlines

The lifeline of polio:

1580   First evidence of polio

1909   Polio confirmed as a virus

1916   Outbreak in New York

1921   Franklin D. Roosevelt contracts polio

1928   The first use of the iron lung

1938   March of Dimes is founded

1948   My case begins

1949   Mower County case, Peg (Schultz) Kehret and 42,833 other cases nationally reported

1952   Sister Kenny comes to the United States and uses hot-pack therapy

1953   Jonas Salk's polio vaccine is given to the masses

1970   Albert Sabin's oral polio vaccine is developed

1985   Rotary launches the Polio Plus program

2003   Peru has one case of polio

2011   Rotary International is still working to eradicate polio

Headlines in local newspapers:

"A strong eighteen year old farm boy living west of Brownsdale, Minnesota was ready to enlist in the Army in 1940. Then he got a headache …"

"In late summer 1952 Dr. Mulder and others had to make hard decisions. Rooms at St. Mary's Hospital in Rochester, Minnesota were full and parents were bringing more and more children."

"The epidemic of 1952 was one of the worst in the Century," *Rochester Post Bulletin* reports.

"Mower County reports yet another case of poliomyelitis. An infant six months old was taken to St. Mary's in October 1948 for polio treatments."

"A young girl of seven in 1930 was reported being treated for polio from Brownsdale, Minnesota."

I was one of these headlines. I am the six-month-old taken to St. Mary's by young parents. My parents were told to just take me to St. Mary's since they couldn't refuse care; if they called in advance, the hospital would say they were too full, and they'd have to go to Minneapolis.

My Story

It is fall, a time of thanksgiving for the bountiful harvest that God has given our farming community, and for the beauty of the season with its amazing color, zest, and brightness. As things slow down, we can stay inside and warm our souls. It will take me a few days to prepare the Thanksgiving feast, so I start on Monday and accomplish a little every day. The feast will be served on Thursday, and my family will join Nolan and me for the day. I have learned over the years that if I get something started, then it will get finished. It always takes a long time to accomplish something worth finishing, so I start early. That is sort of how this project is getting started. The information that will appear in this book has been going around in my head and heart for many years, and it seems that now is the right time to start. I realize that I have things I want to accomplish in my life, so I push on. Good: pushing on is what keeps me going but hard on my body. Bad: I don't want to realize that I push too hard. For you see, I am just beginning my fall years, and the days and years are going faster than I want them to, so I must get projects started if I am going to finish. It has been pointed out to me that November is National Novel Writing Month, so this is the perfect time to move forward with *All the Steps I Have Taken.*

There was no vaccine for polio when I was born in 1948. The worst years of the epidemic were from 1947 to 1953; each year, more children and adults were stricken. Mothers avoided taking their children to any public place, fearing they would become ill. Like most illnesses, polio started with a suggestion that a cold or flu was beginning. As the days progressed, it became evident that the situation was more serious. It didn't matter the person's age; polio attacked the nerve pulp horns and paralyzed them. It could affect arms, legs, or the entire body in a short time. Polio was very contagious, and that is why the fear of taking children to public places such as county fairs or swimming pools came about.

The story as told by my parents was that they decided to go to a farm auction in a nearby town, Wells, Minnesota. It was fall, and the fear of contracting the virus was probably not an issue; it was believed that polio did its best job in the hot and humid summer months. I, six months old, was left home with my grandparents and my sister, Lonna, who was two and a half years older. My mother was an avid seamstress, and a sewing machine was available at the auction. My father, a farmer, was probably interested in a piece of farm machinery. Farm machinery was the main offering at this auction, but the sewing machine was probably on the sale bill as well. They purchased the sewing machine, and my mother was in her glory.

From that day on, I'm sure things were normal until I came down with a fever. The fever didn't let up. For a week, my parents took me every day to see the Doctor in the small town of Blooming Prairie, Minnesota, The symptoms were getting worse. My dad was twenty-four years old and my mom was twenty-three years old when I became ill and they were very worried about my health at the time. I'm sure it was a challenge for them to have a child so small seriously ill, not knowing what to do and not getting answers from the Doctor they trusted to help them make decisions.

Many times over the last few years, I've said to my father, "Tell me about that day I got sick." I always get the same answer. Here is the story, as told by my father: At age twenty-four, he was a young farmer in the Corning area near Austin, Minnesota. It was October, and harvesting corn was probably the only thing on his mind. I'm sure my mother was in charge of caring for the home and family. My sister was strong and healthy, so life for her was pretty carefree and she was always busy playing. Life for me was about to change dramatically. I was going to transform from a normal six-month-old, perhaps sitting up well and just beginning to crawl, into the next polio victim. When my mother took me to Dr. Curtain, the local doctor, that day in October of 1948, he said he suspected what the problem was but couldn't be sure. He said I should be taken to Rochester, Minnesota, forty-five miles away from my family farm. Minneapolis/St. Paul was a hundred miles away. The doctor wanted me at Rochester, closer to my parents' home. He told my parents that so many polio cases were being reported every day that the hospitals were overcrowded; if they called Rochester, the hospital would say I had to be taken to Minneapolis. But so many polio victims were being taken there that no more rooms were available. My mother headed for the field and told my father that they had to take me to Rochester immediately. His heart sank, and he worried that what he'd thought was happening was becoming a reality.

On that beautiful autumn day, my journey began. I would never get the chance to walk, run, skip, jump, dance, or be normal in the ways you think of as normal. For the rest of my life, walking would be a challenge. The choice is mine every day how I will handle that challenge. For a long time now, I've started every day with a prayer for all the patience

I can muster to get me through my day. Some days are very easy to get started, and some days it may take prayer after prayer to get my mind to cooperate with my body. Some days are just plain hard to get started. It doesn't happen often, but sometimes a day comes when I just don't care if I get it started or not.

Polio patients were taught in physical therapy that to be normal we would have to keep up with the rest of the world. I have many projects going on a daily basis, which keeps my mind from being idle; when my mind is idle navigating through my day becomes difficult, because I have time to feel that this is not fun. I don't want that feeling creeping into my mind. Life is good, and I need always to keep that thought foremost in my mind. Life is wonderful, and for that I am so thankful.

The day my mom came to that neighbor's field, a neighbor boy of six years old was there with his father, who was helping with my father's harvest. That young boy, Gary Braaten, now a grown man, goes to my church, Red Oak Grove Lutheran Church, a small country church. All the families in the area go to that church. When having morning coffee with him one Sunday, I asked if I could ask him a few questions about the day my father had to leave the field. He said, "I was just a small boy, not much older than you." He remembered that his parents had been talking about it at the supper table, and I suppose other neighbors had talked about it as well. He said he was old enough to understand the seriousness of the situation and that all the farmers were very concerned. My journey to St. Mary's Hospital in Rochester started the long process of making my life manageable.

I recently contacted the patient affairs office of the Mayo Clinic in Rochester, Minnesota, and had my records sent to me. My admittance day was October 1, 1948. It is interesting to read the handwritten notes from that first day, assessing me as a patient. The chief complaint was fussiness and a temperature of 101.4°F. According to the St. Mary's Hospital medical notes, "She sits up and gets up on her hands and knees. Patient was well until twelve days ago. On September 25, baby became cross and restless. On September 26 was feverish, face flushed, refused food, wanted to sleep a lot, and local doctor prescribed sulfa for infected throat and swollen glands. Arm reflexes present, possible stiffness in neck and back. Later that day cried when her legs were moved. Today when local doctor examined baby she didn't move her left leg." The diagnosis: polio.

That's the beginning of *All the Steps I Have Taken*. As my parents have told me, I was a patient there for a long time. My parents had to stay outside the isolation ward and look at me only through a window for many weeks. I can't imagine the fear they had, as well as the fear those young nurses had while they took care of us patients. When I was at a Triennial Convention for the Evangelical Lutheran Church of America in Philadelphia some years back, I had the opportunity to visit with a nurse who'd been in that situation. We stood by each other in the choir, and every chance we had, she would tell me about her fear. "It was awful," she said. "There were so many of you, and all ages, and the nursery was so full." The nurse had small children at home and worried that she would transport the virus home to her family. I can't imagine the fear she had to deal with; yet she was a dedicated nurse, and her job was to take care of all the sick little ones. She said she prayed every day that her children would not get the virus from her.

My first stay lasted until July of 1949. A body cast was made in June, which I was supposed to wear at night to help with hip deformities. I still have that cast in my collection of items. At that time, my parents arranged for outpatient care. I returned in December for observation, and notes say I had to be readmitted for treatment. I was seen at the Mayo Clinic on February 22, 1950, for an examination and readmitted on February 26, 1950, for right-foot tendon transplant surgery. Notes say that at that time I didn't stand-alone or walk alone but did walk by holding onto furniture. Doctors said "I was a cheerful child in no distress." I guess I was adjusting to my new situation quite nicely. I had surgery on February 27, 1950. This was my second birthday. A month later, the cast and sutures were removed. The cast was made bivalved (cut in half lengthwise) so it could be worn only at night by holding in place with a wrap bandage. A below-the-knee brace was made for the right foot, and physical therapy was suggested. On March 23, 1950, my parents decided that since we lived fifty miles away, they were willing to leave me as a patient in the hospital again, since the doctors thought it was time to teach me to walk. The notes don't say how long I stayed for physical therapy. When I returned for a checkup in November, the rehabilitation notes say that I was walking fairly well. My muscle power was not changing, and the tendon transplant was healing nicely. There was talk of a long leg brace for the left leg to help with the back knee.

My grandparents and sister could visit only on Sundays when I was hospitalized. I don't remember them coming, but I have pictures that my mother saved for me, and now I have compiled a wonderful memory book. I have pictures that show me in a big wooden wheelchair outside on the lawn with my family. I also have pictures of me in a crib with my crib partner, and another of us in one of those big wooden wheelchairs together at St. Mary's Hospital. My crib partner was Ginny Goldberg from Austin, and we spent time together after she was admitted to St. Mary's on October 10, 1949. She recently received her medical records from Mayo. She had no pictures or information about her experience and was very happy when we met and I showed her some pictures of her. She said, "I read through some of it, and it made me want to cry. I can't believe I went through all that. I can't imagine how my parents dealt with all the health problems."

After the muscles were damaged, the hard work of therapy began, with the goal of regaining whatever mobility was possible. My memory goes back only to about the age of six or seven. I remember that every February or March my parents had an appointment at the Mayo Clinic, and the doctors would discuss my progress and decide what option was best for me. My father said that many times, they would look at him and my mother and say, "We are not sure what to do." But they knew they had to do something to try to better my mobility, so they would schedule a surgery for the week after school was dismissed for the summer. I would get one week of summer vacation and then become a patient again. I'd spend two weeks or more in the hospital, healing and getting a cast, and then I'd go home to heal further. Many times the surgery was for one of my feet. It didn't matter which one; whichever needed the most urgent attention would be operated on. I'd spend the rest of the summer on crutches.

Despite the crutches, I was still able to get to the top of the corncrib, which was where we had a playhouse. We would build all our furniture and cupboards out of wooden peach crates left from my mothers canning. Climbing up wasn't very easy, but my arms were strong, and the slivers I got in my knees as I pulled myself up there were easy to get out. What fun we had!

I spent almost every summer during grade school in a cast, mending and hoping I would be rid of all the casts and crutches in time to go back to school in the fall as a normal child. This went on each summer until I was able to rid myself of the last brace. I definitely remember the fall of my sophomore year. The surgery I underwent that summer was for an astragular arthrodesis, or triple ankle fusion, of my left ankle. It was dreadful. This surgery was completed at Gillette State Hospital for Crippled Children in St. Paul. My parents had arranged with Mayo to transfer my care so they could get more financial help. This surgery was very painful, and getting rid of those crutches was impossible. I simply couldn't make myself do it. I became dependent on those crutches to get myself around. It was too hard to walk with a stiff, painful ankle, and it was impossible to hide such a significant limp. Using the crutches was faster, and I didn't walk funny. The crutches became part of my version of normal. I got on the bus just fine at the end of the sidewalk. Because of my limitations, my siblings were at an advantage for the bus, because it came into our farmyard and turned around so I didn't have to walk down the long driveway. They thought that was fantastic. We could wait in the house until the bus came up into the yard and then walk out to the end of the sidewalk. When I got to school, my friend Barb would meet me and carry my books, because I had the crutches to contend with. My day was great. Barb and I would leave every class three minutes early so we could change books and get to the next class on time. I would be dismissed early at the end of the day so I could get to the bus on time for the ride home.

Everything was going great until the day my father took those crutches away. Can you believe he did that? I was devastated, and I was so angry with my dad. How could he think that would help me? Now I was back to taking tiny steps with that awful limp, and everyone could see me walking so crazily. It was impossible to stop crying. How would I ever get on that bus and get through my school day? I still got out of each class early, but now I got to the next class late, because it took me so long to get there. I almost missed the bus at the end of the day, because it was the first one in the bus line and a long walk from the door of the school. Barb felt terrible; she could no longer be my helper. I was sixteen years old, disappointed and defeated. I'm sure I thought it was the end of the world. It took a few days to realize that my father had done just what he should have done. He pushed me back into the mode of doing all I could for myself to become normal again. It wasn't long before I was making the best of every day and thanking him for giving me the push I needed at that time in my life. This surgery was the one that got rid of my last brace. I had worn braces all my life on one or both legs, and now I was rid of them forever.

I began to learn that my destiny is tied to the decisions I make every day as to how I begin and end each day. It is all about choices. We can choose to make our days anything we would like them to be. I try to live my life as a canvas, putting all the color I can into it. I am a quilter, and I see how the beautiful colors blend together, and I know I can do that with my life every day. I weave in faith, and God finds the thread. I use four P's as guidelines for weaving a rich and colorful life: prayer, prioritize, patience, and persistence. Each day must start with time to pray. This is when I read my Thomas Kinkade devotional book and have my first cup of coffee. Then it is time to prioritize the things that are most important and will need to be completed today. Then comes patience. It's hard to be patient when you want to get a lot completed, and I work slowly, so patience is an absolute must. I remind myself all day long to be patient. It is very hard to do, but it seems that the older I get, the easier it is. Persistence is just sticking with the project until it is completed. I'll always get the job done if I get it started. It is my own fault if I start too many things in one day and then get frustrated that I didn't get them all done. I used to make a list of things to do and then cross each item off. But then it got so that too many things were not completed on the list, so I don't make lists anymore. I simply stay focused and get done what I can.

Today is a new day, and I see white on the ground. That means snow has arrived, and that means that it will be slippery outside. I wait until the last minute to bring my boots up from the basement. Once snow is on the ground, I make careful decisions about when I leave the house and where I go. My greatest fear is falling. Once I'm dressed and ready for my day, I use a cane for extra balance, but it doesn't help much if I'm on ice or snow. In the house, the cane stays by the back door unless my back is very tired and I need the extra support. Only the most important things can get me out into the snow. When I needed to get to work, there was no choice. I just got as close to the door of the dental office as I could, and if someone was coming to work at the same time, he or she always offered me an arm; I never turn down a helping arm. On many of my workdays, my husband and I rode together, so I would get dropped off and picked up at the back door of the office. This was very helpful. The car was always warm when I got picked up on those cold winter days.

The snow is so beautiful, but many things were more difficult for me to do in the winter. Our children got to spend extra time with their father while learning to ice skate. The older ones helped the younger ones as time went on. I loved to go sledding until I had so many bionic parts that the possibility of hurting myself felt too risky; it would be too costly to damage some part of my body and have to go through surgery and recovery all over again. I no longer partake in any dangerous activity. It's difficult to get back up the hill now, so I just stay at the top and watch. A fabulous winter day is best enjoyed with a horse-drawn sleigh ride with friends and family. Or I sit by the window, watch it snow, and enjoy a great book. I just change the activity a bit and still enjoy the beauty of winter. It is a good time to get a fire going and watch a good movie or sew on a quilt.

Footsteps and Braces

Shoes must protect feet. I have never been able to go barefoot, so I don't know the feeling of having sand or grass between my toes. When I was a young child, my right foot was larger than my left, so buying shoes was expensive; I got only one pair per year. Actually, I got two pairs—I needed one size to fit the left foot and one to fit the right. One of the shoe stores in Austin, Minnesota, Smith's Shoe Store, was wonderful. They tried so hard to fit me with something I would like. The choices were very few, since I had to have shoes that tied, with lots of support, since my braces would be attached to them. They sound becoming, don't they? The ones that usually worked were boys' shoes in brown. The fact that I needed two sizes, and that braces would be attached to the soles, made such shoes very unattractive for a little girl. Remember, though, that I knew nothing different. This was how it always was, because I had only one pair. The toes would be worn right through by the time I was ready for new shoes and new braces the next year.

Buying shoes is still a very difficult and disappointing task. However, at least I can avoid buying two sizes by using an insole in the left or right shoe, whichever I need. In 1983, I had to return to the use of a brace on my left leg to support my knee. In my left leg there are no tendons, ligaments or muscles strong enough to hold the knee in place, so at age thirty-six, I had to rely once again on the support of a brace. I was scheduled for arthroscopic surgery to see if anything could be done for the knee. After surgery I found out that nothing could be done and that I'd have to wear a brace to support it. After the doctor left my room, I called my husband to let him know I was ready to leave the hospital but that we had to stop at the brace shop so I could get fitted for a long left leg brace. This was very difficult to adjust to, since I'd been without brace support for twenty years. But I knew that if I didn't go *that* day, I might have never decided to have the brace made. This was another hard decision. While I was waiting for the brace to be made I needed to use my crutches following the surgery. At church the following Sunday a wonderful woman, Eileen Kittelson, encouraged me by saying, "You did it before when you were little, and you can do it again." This was true, but I didn't *want* to do it again. I had spent enough time in braces.

Now I have two different braces to support my left knee. One goes all the way into my left shoe; and I had the other one, I used in a Mayo brace test, was made to stop at my ankle so that I can wear nicer-looking shoes and maybe sandals in the summer. To decide which brace to wear, I must think about what I am going to be accomplishing during the day and then determine what brace is best. The long leg brace, which goes all the way from my thigh to my toes, is much sturdier and more durable. I'll wear this one if I want to do a lot of walking or something that takes a lot of energy. This is the one I wore to work every day. The other brace is smaller and allows me to wear regular shoes while still supporting my knee. But I can't do a lot of standing and walking with this brace. Therefore, I need different shoes for each brace. The long brace takes up space in my shoe, so the shoes I decide to wear are half a size bigger to accommodate for the brace. Then I have to tighten up the right shoe with an insole and a lift. Both of my ankles are fused, so it is very hard to find shoes with the right heel height. If I find shoes that are good for the left foot, they will be too low for the right, and the same way the other way around. If they are good for the left, then I have to have the right one built up or wear a lift.

This was confirmed for me recently when I went on a mission to find shoes of a certain style from ten years ago. I had worn these shoes until they looked like I shouldn't wear them anymore, but I wouldn't give them up. They work for both feet and are comfortable. So my husband and I went on a day trip to find them. They were Red Wing brand shoes, made in Red Wing, Minnesota. We made the journey and found the shoe-repair shop where I'd bought them, but the shop no longer sold Red Wing seconds. They said I would have to go to the basement of the Red Wing store. They had a couple of pairs of tennis shoes in both of the sizes I needed, so I bought two discontinued pairs. I wear them a lot, since they adapt easily to my needs. I was so excited, because now I have a pair to wear with either brace. The owners of the shoe store then directed me to the basement of the Red Wing shoe store, and the number of shoes overwhelmed me. Surely I would be able to find some shoes that would fit. After two hours of trying on shoes that I thought would work with the shorter brace, I found stylish shoes in black and brown, and I was set. I needed to have the left one made lower on one pair and the right one made higher on the second pair. The shoe-repair store was closing in twenty minutes, so we headed back. I walked in, ready for the clerk to make notes on what needed to be done. I would return to pick them up or have them sent to me. The excitement was mounting. I took the first pair out of the box, and he looked at the heel and said "he couldn't do anything"; he said "the heel was probably hollow, and if he cut into it, he would damage the shoe." I took the other pair out of the box, and he said the same thing. After the excitement of finding them, disappointment set in; they were not going to work. I had to take them both back. On the bright side, I did get two pairs of the same tennis shoes in the two sizes I needed, and the steps I take will be many. I can get a new outfit or two in blue and gray, so they will really match. I'll be all set to take lots of steps in comfort and style—at least, as stylish as I can get.

Steps as a Daughter

My mother was the hardest-working woman I knew. She was of German descent and one of six children. She had four older brothers and one younger sister. Two brothers were in the war, one of which never returned. The other two brothers never married and stayed on the farm to help my Grandpa. Work was all they knew. From a very young age, my mother weeded in the onion fields of Hollandale, Minnesota. She worked in the hemp factory during the war before becoming a farmer's wife and continuing the hard work on the farm. Her duties on the farm were endless, and she held down a job off the farm as well. She was the one who made sure we had new clothes, which she sewed, and food on the table, which she grew in the garden and then canned.

I will never forget those summer days of sitting in the basement, stemming and cutting beans until the Band-Aids on our thumbs didn't help anymore. Her magic number was one hundred: a hundred jars of corn, green beans, yellow beans, peaches, tomatoes, meat, and pickles, processed and put on the shelves in the basement. My sister did the picking, and we younger ones prepared for the processing, which included washing all the jars and getting the items ready to put into the jars. This food tasted so good in the middle of winter. Feeding our family of seven, which included dad, mom, Lonna, me, Patricia, Timothy and Daniel was possible thanks to her ability to do all these things. All the farm women worked hard like this. It was the normal way of life. My mother-in-law was just as hard a worker, providing for her family of eight, which included, Nolan's father, Lawrence and his mother, Mildred. Nolan's family also included L. Dean, Marlys, Diane, Douglas, Nolan and Terry. These wonderful women were also very active in their communities and churches. My mother and mother-in-law died from cancer when they were sixty and sixty-one, respectively. They could have taught me much more had I had the opportunity to enjoy them longer. My mother spent six long years battling cancer. My sister recently told me that she asked our mother how she could battle for so long and with such courage. Her response was that she learned how to be courageous from watching me do all the things I had to do to overcome my own challenges. It is magnificent to realize that I helped her during her time of need without even being aware of it. She was courageous and never complained. My dad, siblings and I took care of her for six years in her home. We had three young children at the time, we both had jobs, and we were insanely busy. Nonetheless, my husband was so helpful. We could never have gotten through those years without cooperating.

My father was the youngest of three children. He had one older sister and one older brother. His ancestors were Swedish and Danish. When my father was twelve his parents divorced and he continued living on the farm. I always remember him telling me how he started farming at a very young age, probably when he was twelve. He was a good farmer, tending to the land with crops of hay, corn, and beans. He was one of the first in the area in the 1960s to have a milking parlor, which could accommodate eight cows at one time, four on each side. People came from all over to see his dairy operation. He was so proud of that. Along with the dairy and crops he managed to raise pigs. Mom had the chickens. I do remember him getting away on deer hunting trips and smelt fishing trips. My younger brother Danny eventually helped in the dairy operation. When he decided he would rather go into construction work instead of working on a farm the cows were sold. That was a sad day when the auction for selling those cows was over. All my siblings had jobs on the farm. Lonna and Patty helped rake hay and helped with the baling. I generally helped with feeding all the helpers on the farm and spent my time in the kitchen. It was safer for me working in the house. I had begged and begged to rake hay over and over again but my dad just wouldn't let me. He knew it would be too hard for me. Finally the day came when I could give it a try. I was so excited. I got up on that tractor ready to get the field ready for afternoon baling and it didn't take me one time around the field to realize that dad was probably right. It was a bigger job than I could handle with the clutch on my left side. I finished one round and said "that was enough." At least I was given the opportunity to try for myself. At the time of my mother's death, my father decided he would move into town and sell the farm. He is now eighty-six years old, and my siblings and I are helping him very little through health issues and ensuring that he has a good quality of life. He and his companion, Helen, have very good days together, and we are grateful that they have each other. They so dearly enjoy each other's companionship.

Steps as a Registered Dental Assistant: My Career

We all dream of what we want to be when we grow up. If you ask a small child what he or she wants to be when they grow up, you usually get an answer. Of course, it will change six times before it's time to pursue a career. After being a patient so many times during my younger years, I decided that nursing would be perfect for me. However, the reality of nursing simply wouldn't work for me, since I probably wouldn't be able to be on my feet for so much of the day. My next great idea was to become a hairdresser. I loved fixing my maternal grandmother's beautiful silver-gray hair in pin curls every week, and she always combed it out so pretty the next day. It was great fun for Grandpa and Grandma to come to our home every week to have supper and I would pin curl my grandmother's hair. My paternal grandmother lived on our farm in a small house, and I always cut her hair. Her natural curls made it easy to cut, and she always loved how it turned out—at least, that was what she always told me. Hairdressing would be perfect for me. Again, however, I came to my senses and realized that I would be on my feet all day. Now what was I going to do?

Something had to be out there for me—something I could benefit from, something with which I could make a living. I had to make a decision. I wanted to help people better their health in someway. I decided that Dental Assisting would be for me. I had visited with the guidance councilor at my high school to help with the decision. I would attend Brainerd Area Vocational School in the fall of 1967 to study dental assisting. My choices at the time were Mankato College in Mankato, Minnesota, or the University of Minnesota in Minneapolis, Minnesota, and Brainerd Area Vocational College. Mankato and the University were much larger than I wanted. Brainerd Area Vocational College was starting to train for four-handed dentistry, and I would be able to sit and assist the dentist. Our class would be the college's first graduating class in dental assisting. It would be wonderful. I would be able to help people better their health by teaching good dental care. School was fantastic, except for the fact that I was a long way from home and became very homesick. In those days, young people didn't have access to cars like they do now. I rode my bike to the school until the snow fell, and then I rode with the woman I lived with. The year went quickly, and I studied hard. Soon I got my first dental assistant job, in St. Paul, and I was on my own. A dental assisting classmate and I lived together. I was employed in five offices over the next forty-two years. It was a rewarding professional career, and I loved it.

As the years went by, my body started to show wear and tear. After completing a medical examination by my doctor, she referred me to a physical therapist. He suggested that I should use a cane. I'd been told the same thing when I was fifteen years old, when I was trying so hard to get rid of those crutches and braces. Why would I have wanted to use a cane? That would have been so degrading. But now, in my late fifties, I had the sense to let it help me. My therapist said, "If you only use it 25 percent of the time, then you will be 25 percent less tired at the end of your day." This was true, but now I had another adjustment

All the Steps I Have Taken

to contend with. My employers, Doctors Elrod, Green, and Hyland, were fine with the idea, and I worked with and without my cane during the final years of my career. It was hard to carry surgical trays with a cane in one hand, so sometimes I would use it and sometimes not, but I made it through each day.

I had an awakening in the summer of 2007 when my back became very stressed and painful and I was off work for ten days. My doctor suggested that I consider not working anymore. I wasn't ready to make that decision. I got better and was more careful about doing difficult tasks. I would limit myself to working on a project for only two hours and then do something else. What do I want to get accomplished? This is where choices have to be made. What is priority? Every thing went great until 2009, when I was working extra for people on vacation. The extra money would help with our upcoming vacation to Deadwood, South Dakota. The weather was great, the road trip was fantastic, and we enjoyed time with friends. I returned to work after our vacation feeling not quite the way I should have. My back was really tired, and it got so painful that one day I put my crutches in the car just in case I needed them. Since I limp to the left, the right side of my back suffers. This wasn't always the case, and I am so thankful that my back was able to stand the stress I put on it for as long as I did.

I made it through that Monday and Tuesday at work with the help of Dr. Bobee Hyland. On Tuesday, I explained to her that I was in extreme pain and that I'd make it through the day, but only with her help. I said that she would have to help me help her take care of the patients scheduled for that day. I explained to her that I had my crutches in the car and asked her to be the runner if I forgot something or needed different instruments. She asked why I was at work that day, and I explained that I had Wednesday and Thursday off; I would use those days to rest my back, and all would be fine. I did not like to admit that it was difficult for me and hardly ever asked for help, but that day I desperately needed help, and she obliged. I made it through that Tuesday, and that was the last day I worked as a registered dental assistant.

I did take the two days off. I spent them with my daughter Lianna and her two children at her camper, which had been previously planned; I didn't want to disappoint the kids or myself. She had some vacation days and was going to enjoy them at her camper. Her husband was not camping with us, so I drove to Wisconsin after work and tried to rest. I tried to cover up the pain and enjoy the time with the kids. By the end of Wednesday, however, Addison and Aden were not enjoying the cool, rainy weather, and I wasn't enjoying the discomfort. At supper that night, we all decided it was best to head home. I thought I should see my doctor and make sure things were all right with my hip and back. We asked the kids what they thought, and they also wanted to go home. So we gave up our camping day together and headed home. On the drive home, with Lianna and the kids in the car ahead of me, I had lots to think about. I knew it was time to make that final decision. My son, Aaron, called me while I was driving, and I had a hard time not crying; my decision weighed on my mind, and I was in great pain. He said "I didn't have to prove anything to anyone. I had spent my life up to that point doing just that." On that fall day in September 2009, I had to make the hardest decision I will ever make in my life. It was far more difficult than deciding that I wanted to be married to my loving husband and far more difficult than deciding to become a mother. I had to retire after forty-two years, giving up a career that had been rewarding, satisfying, and an adequate source of income for my family.

I have always spent my time doing things that are possible for me to do and doing them well. I really do not look at things that I cannot do; rather, I focus on the things I can do and enjoy. I'd begun to think about retiring at the end of 2008. At my performance review, in January of 2009, I decided that the end of 2009 would be the end of my professional career. I knew I had to come to grips with the fact that I could no longer be on my feet and do all the walking and carrying my work required. My co-workers were so awesome. They helped with tasks that were difficult for me. They would no longer let me get things from the basement; they would run and get them for me. If I were scheduled to be in the lab for the day, they would share the day with me so I wouldn't have to stand all day. I appreciated it so much, and they were wonderful about it, but it helped me realize that I simply couldn't pull my weight anymore. That wasn't fair to the rest of the staff. A replacement would be found for my position. I even helped by suggesting someone I knew.

The year 2009 was going well. My replacement would start in October of 2009 following her maternity leave whenever she was ready. When I made my decision in 2008 to be ready to retire in 2009 I suggested that the time line be adjustable. When someone could start I would be flexible to retire. I was starting to dread October. I did not want to count down the days, and I would be very sad to leave, but it was my decision, and I was really trying to muddle through it. I'd had some problems with my back a few years before that, so I knew I had to be careful. However, the day came when those crutches were in the car. I'd had a hip replacement, and the pain up the side of my right leg into my back was so intense that I needed to make sure the hip was fine. My doctor, Dr. Carol Holtz, had suggested in 2007 that I not work anymore. It was simply too hard on my body. On that second day off, the day after we came home, I had another doctor's appointment, and Dr. Holtz simply looked at me very seriously and said, "Now are you ready to refrain from work?" I had to admit that this time I really was ready to finish. This time it was God making the pain and discomfort so bad that I had to make the choice to not continue to push myself. I had been given plenty of opportunities to make that decision in the past, but I would always get better and then just be more careful and get along fine. This time the message was clear. I simply had to say I was ready to finish my career.

It was so hard for me to say I wasn't going to be able to work anymore. I called the office and simply said that I would not be returning until Friday after 2:00, when they finished their workday, to clean out my locker. They knew I'd been in pain on Monday and Tuesday, so it really wasn't a surprise that I would not be returning to my job. I arrived at 2:30 when I thought they would all be done and gone. However, they were still working. They all said, "We didn't want to be here when you came to clean out your locker." It was good to see them and receive a hug from each and tell them all "good bye". By that time, I had adjusted to the fact that I really was making the right decision. My children said, "Mom, it's really the time that you start thinking more about what's best for you." I thought I'd been doing this all along, but really I'd just wanted to keep pushing forward. I didn't want to be a quitter, but God put a strong enough block in front of me. This time I couldn't get around it. I had to stop. The office had a very nice retirement party for me, and I was able to get up and tell them how much I enjoyed being part of that staff for ten and a half years. It was easy for me to say something nice about every one of my coworkers. I loved every day I spent with them.

Steps to Being a Sibling

I am the second of five children. I have already spoken about my older sister, Lonna, who came to visit me at the hospital. She was always smarter than me. She played the piano better than me. We grew up on a farm, and we had to work to help the family get things done. We raised chickens and pigs and milked dairy cows. We grew up not being afraid of work. I was usually in charge of gathering eggs. I became deathly afraid of the chickens, because when I went into the henhouse, it didn't take long before they started pecking at the metal on my braces. When they missed, they pecked the skin, which hurt. If I was in the farmyard and the chickens saw me, I usually had to get to the swing set and up on the monkey bar as quickly as I could, or they would try to peck at me again. I couldn't get there very fast, so I usually got a peck or two. Soon I just didn't want to be anywhere around those chickens, and Lonna would gather the eggs. I had to sit in the basement and wash them.

Lonna was a leader and did everything well. She was a cheerleader, and I admired her. I could never do that. She was in the class plays, while I didn't want to be in front of anyone and draw attention to myself. She was our homecoming queen in my freshman year. To this day, she is very forward and involved. She and her family live near Owatonna, Minnesota. We enjoy time together. She is involved with Rotary International, an organization that has given millions of dollars to eradicating polio. Lonna has two grown children and four grandchildren.

My younger sister, Patricia Lynn, felt like there was never enough time left for her in the family. She had me just ahead of her and our brother Timothy just after her. Being a middle child, she felt she always got leftovers of time. Our parents were so busy with Timothy and me that she was probably right. If she wasn't with me up in the playhouse, she was off by herself with her kittens. If we couldn't find her on the farmyard, we would simply call the dog; wherever the dog came from was where Patty could be found. The better part of her day would be following dad around outside anywhere on the farm. She has many talents with knitting and flower gardening being two of her passions that she enjoys. Animals are still a big part of her life. A career in teaching was her professional calling. She works with special-needs children and young adults helping them find their way in the world. She recently received a wonderful award for the work she does with her special-needs kids. She lives in Blaine, Minnesota, and has two grown children.

My brother Timothy arrived on November 14, 1955. We three girls were so happy to have a baby brother. He was lucky to have three older sisters for babysitters. Lonna, was born in 1945, I was born in 1948 and Patricia was born in 1951. Our mother was a very hard worker, as I mentioned earlier, and I know she welcomed the extra care we gave Timothy. She worked on and off the farm to provide a good life for us. Her jobs were endless. We all learned to be part of that plan, and we all had jobs to take care of. This little boy was loved, but Timothy Dean was to be with us for only a very short time. I loved him so much, and we spent a lot of time together. In his baby book, my mother wrote in her notes regarding his birth, "He looks a lot like Linda." He did look just like me as a baby. At the young age of three, he had a very serious kidney infection and spent time in the hospital. He spent a lot of time at the doctor. My parents had two children who required a lot of care and expense. And then the fifth child, Daniel, was born when Timmy was two. Our family was complete.

We all worked hard to make the farm a great place to live. Timmy was so happy doing all the things little boys do. When he felt well, he played so hard. He loved to put worms in his pockets. He always told me he felt sorry for me because of the way I walked. Little did he know that with his constant kidney and bladder infections his situation was more serious than my physical challenges. Though he was always sick, he was simply the sweetest little boy, and he enjoyed all he could when he felt healthy. His favorite activity was Sunday school, and his favorite song was "Jesus Loves Me." Our grandmother lived in a small house on our farm, and we all spent lots of time there, playing games with her. Timothy spent many days there playing those games.

In June of 1961, Timmy was hospitalized with a congenital disease; he had an obstruction in the vessel of the bladder and advanced kidney damage. He had worn a catheter from a very young age to help drain his bladder. Now things were growing more serious for little Timmy. His doctor changed the catheter every month or whenever he had an infection. Our mother had her hands full, to say the least. I continued having surgeries every year; she had a large family to look after; she had a home on a farm to run; and she worked outside the home as well. I am not sure how she did all that.

In early September of 1962, Timmy was planning to go to kindergarten. He was so excited. I can still see him in his tan pants, striped shirt,

31

and tan sweater, holding his book bag, going off to school with us on the bus. He hadn't been feeling well, and though our mother thought he should wait until he felt better to go to school, he wouldn't hear of it. He was going to go to school. He made it through the whole first day and half of the second. Then he got so sick he had to go to the hospital again. The doctors at St. Mary's said simply that nothing could be done to help him. The damage was far too severe, and no medical options were available. My parents brought him home, and he was with us during those last days. He stayed in my parents' bed, and we all spent time with him, rubbing his swollen stomach to help with the pain. He said to all of us that Jesus was his nearest and dearest friend and that he would relieve him of this terrible pain and make him new. He prayed that prayer every minute of those last days. He passed away with his parents, siblings, and grandparents with him on September 10, 1962. He was six years, ten months, and ten days old. He had such strong faith in the few years he lived, and I think of him almost every day. What a blessing he was to all of us. I look forward to meeting him again in my eternal life.

Daniel William was now the little brother we adored. We all enjoyed his basketball games; however, we made him so nervous that he asked us not to come. After all the girls had left home, he was the only child remaining. It was like being an only child. Our parents finally were able to remodel the old farmhouse. They finally could afford a big project like that. He dairy farmed with our father for many years before he decided it was not the work he wanted to do for the rest of his life. He changed professions and went on to work in construction. He and his wife, Diane, live near Lansing, Minnesota. They have two grown sons.

Responses from Siblings

I recently asked my siblings to write something about "Living with Linda."

Response from My Sister Lonna:

I was the firstborn of five children, with Linda two and a half years behind me. Since I was so young when it happened, I don't remember what life was like when polio paralyzed her from the waist down when she was six months old. Those memories have been created from the many photos that were taken and put into albums. When I realized that our mother had to drive to Rochester every day for fourteen months straight, I asked what she did with me, and her answer was, "I don't remember—I guess you stayed at your grandma's." As I grew up, I concluded that what I did with my life was up to me; I couldn't count on my mother or father. This made me very independent, and I started dreaming about what I wanted my adult life to be while I sat in the one-room County O'Leary schoolhouse. At home, as soon as I was able, I was given responsibility for the family meals, since our mother worked as a waitress and left for work at five o'clock. I was to see to it that the family got fed. Mom usually had supper in the oven when we arrived home from school. I made sure the kitchen was cleaned up.

Then off I would go to practice piano, and then I'd go to my room. I really preferred alone time after being so busy with all the activities on the farm.

Linda's strength and determination to get better always amazed me. She was relentless when it came to meeting her mobility challenges, and she had such a strong desire to get rid of the crutches, braces, and lift on her shoe. Every summer would bring another surgery to improve her mobility. The days, weeks, and even months afterward were challenging, especially with the heat of each day. She was so clever at finding ways to deal with the itching stitches, and she really did not complain. She had playtime with Patricia. I acted more like the eldest I was, doing the domestic work; I was never much of a playing child.

Conventional wisdom says that birth order has a large impact on how personalities evolve in a family, and I do believe this is the case with us. Studies have shown that firstborns seem to have certain unique traits, and I think that is the case with me. Linda's story was a challenge for the family, but it never felt like a burden; she was so determined to reach her goals that it became a family affair to help her. It was always reassuring to see her conquer another milestone, and there was much family pride when she did.

Today, she still never ceases to amaze me with her strong will and determination to get things done. She put the pattern in place at a very young age and marched on with setting goals. She always has many, many, many activities going on in her busy life. I'd say she is a woman driven to get things done. Relaxing or indulging in downtime is not her norm. However, I do believe that during her retirement she will embrace a less-is-more philosophy when it comes to physical and social activities and celebrate her many accomplishments with a huge smile on her face.

Respectfully written by Lonna Jeanne, sister

Response from My Sister Patricia:

I am going to put down some things spontaneously, as they come to mind. You were so determined, adamant that you would be able to do what everyone else could do. That included riding a horse and going bowling; you never wanted to be left out of anything. I felt bad when people stared as you struggled to walk down the streets of Austin, Minnesota. Your shoes would come home from the repair shop and have that thick lift on them. I always felt bad when you had to be in the house with Mom, cleaning; but I liked how you supported her. I just wanted to be outdoors, driving the tractor, following Dad around, and being with the animals. I know it was hard for you to share a room with me. You wanted it nice and neat, and I couldn't maintain that level of tidiness. You were always the one who didn't follow the rules, using the vehicles for a slightly different purpose than you may have told our parents. I remember the hours we spent working on the eggs together in the basement, breaking them and playing catch with the yolks.

You were always so active, always doing something for yourself and others. I would get letters from you in the mail, and I would be exhausted by the time I got to the end, just following all your activities. You were passionate about being a mother and wife and happy that you could have children. You are so talented and devoted to your sewing skills. I loved your determination to play the piano as an adult; you were never one to give up. You are so devoted to your church and religion. I felt badly that school was challenging for you, and I hated what Mr.

Benson expected of you in music class, making you stand without a podium—what were those people thinking? It was hard to see you spending summer after summer in bed after all those surgeries. I felt like it wasn't fair to you. Despite it all, you kept smiling. I felt you got the good looks because of your disability and felt that this was God's plan. You never did anything unless it was done well. I admired your desire to be a camp counselor and enjoyed your interest and love for Camp Courage.

Pat

Response from My Brother Daniel:

A personal interview with Dan revealed that he doesn't remember too much about "living with Linda." I realized that if I called him to ask for this information he probably wouldn't respond. When I graduated from high school and went off to college at Brainerd Vocational College, he was only seven years old. He does recall that I came to see him play basketball, probably with one or two of my children. He says that now I am a woman who gets a lot done.

Thoughts on My Siblings' Responses:

It was very interesting to get my siblings' responses. Although they all made quite similar comments, I was surprised that they had such strong feelings. Yes, I did get an "A" for effort in eighth-grade bowling, just for giving it my best shot. Yes, I did do a few devilish things during my teenage years, but no harm was ever done and I usually didn't get away with it. My dad would check the mileage on the car or pickup, so he knew if I went somewhere other than where I said I was going.

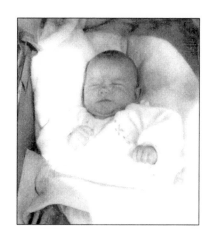

Admittance Day 10-1-48

Lonna and Linda on St. Mary's lawn

Dad and Linda

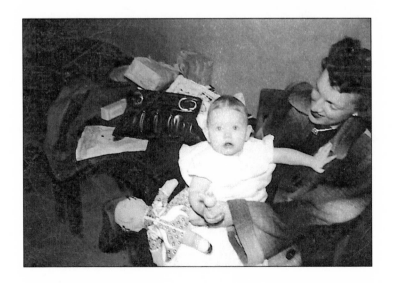

Mom and Linda

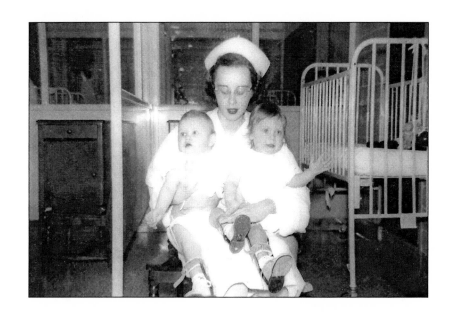

Linda and Ginny Goldberg and unidentified nurse

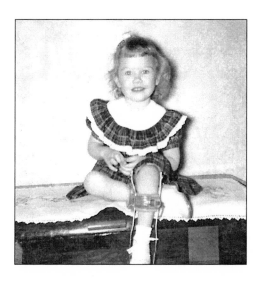

Linda

From left: Lonna, Mom, me holding Daniel, Patricia, Dad, and Timothy

Back row, from left: Bob, Tonya, Jessie, Aaron, Lianna, Cole,
Aden, Travis, Addison
Front row, from left: Ryan, me, Cade, Nolan, Anika, Emma
Not pictured: Cody

Steps to Becoming a Wife

Getting married and having a family were things I always knew I wanted to be a part of my life. I was never very forward and didn't always have strong self-confidence while I was in school. I hated having to stand in front of the class to present a report or for any other reason. I just didn't like being the center of attention. Staying in the background was just fine with me. I always wondered why someone would pick me out of all the pretty girls out there.

My husband, Nolan, and I attended the same high school and the same church, so our paths crossed often. High-school band, school chorus, and church choir were the most likely places where we would be at the same time. He had and still has the most beautiful singing voice, and I guess that was one of the first things I loved about him. And could he dance! All the girls watched him. I wasn't the best in that department, but I gave it the best I could and did have fun with it. Prom was probably our first big date. I was so excited. It was fun dressing up in that pretty pink gown. Pretty dresses need pretty shoes. Which was difficult, but I managed to find a pair of white shoes that could be built up for the left foot, and I was ready for the evening. By the time we got to the dance, which began after dinner, I had such a big blister on the back of my left foot that I found the evening very challenging. I remember having a wonderful time, and I hoped I would spend more time with this young man.

I went off to college, and he finished his senior year and did the things one should do in the last year of high school. People came and went in our lives, and time went on. At one point, I was sure I'd been forgotten. But he hadn't forgotten me. I was living in St. Paul and I would come home on weekends occasionally and we would cross paths. Sometimes I came home on the bus and he picked me up in Blooming Prairie, Minnesota. Our lives reconnected, and our future rekindled. My parents were so happy when we decided to get married. I have always felt sort of lucky that he chose me. I often think about the book *Puppies for Sale* by Dan Clark, (www.danclarkspeak.com) which tells of a little boy who looks in a store window and sees a sign that says "Puppies for sale." He goes inside and tells the store owner that he wants to look at the puppies. He asks how much they are, and the owner tells him $50. The boy has only $2.37, but he asks if he can see them. The puppies come over, but one lags behind. The boy asks what's wrong with him, and the owner says he's missing a hip socket and will always limp like that. That's the one the boy wants to buy. The store owner says, "You don't want to buy that dog. If you really want him I'll give him to you."

The boy comes close to the owner's face and says, "I don't want you to just give him to me. He is worth just as much as all the other puppies and I'll pay the full amount of $50. I'll give you $2.37 now and 50 cents a month until I have him paid for."

"No, no, no," the owner says. "He's never going to be able to run and jump and play like the other dogs."

The boy lifts his pants to reveal a badly twisted right leg supported by two steel braces and says, "Well sir, I don't run so well myself, and the puppy will need someone who understands."

I have always felt blessed that I was chosen, even though I had outward physical limitations and would not be able to run that fast, either. It didn't matter. Nolan loved me anyway, and we have enjoyed forty-three years together. He has some slight medical limitations, and I try to understand how he feels, because I probably have the same ache or pain; we can help each other through our days. He is excellent at helping with anything in our home. He is better in the kitchen than I am and he always enjoys serving a great meal. The kids used to say that I was so lucky to have Dad help me so much. I said, "God did better than just giving me your dad; he gave me three helpful children as well." The kids were always my extra runners when I needed something. On my days off, when I was working in the yard, Aaron would be my helper when he got home from school until he went off to his job for an area farmer.

Nolan and I are both retired and enjoy spending time at our permanent camping area, Eagle Cliff Camp Ground, (www.eagle-cliff.com) each summer near Lanesboro, Minnesota. It is located along the Root River on the bike trail. We enjoy spending time with our children, grandchildren, and friends. My days are filled with grandchildren, sewing alterations, church activities, piano, hardanger embroidery, quilting, games of any kind, biking, camping, watching the Minnesota Twins baseball, lifting my spirit with Ellen DeGeneres, and taking care of our home and flower gardens. I shall never be bored. As long as I can put one foot in front of the other, I will never be uninterested in activity.

Steps to Being a Mother

I come from a family of five children. My husband is from a family of six children. When we were dating, we talked about having a family. It never once entered my mind that I might not be able to have children. Since I'd always thought I was normal, I just never entertained the possibility of not becoming a mother. I didn't realize that my parents were really worried during my first pregnancy. First they doubted whether I could get pregnant, and then they worried about whether I could carry a child. I did just great, though, and experienced the same joy, wonderment, and excitement as any other mother-to-be.

Our daughter, Tonya Beth, was born on July 19, 1972. She was our first miracle. She was the product of a loving marriage and the fulfillment of young love. She came into the world at 9:22 p.m. weighing six pounds twelve ounces and measuring nineteen inches long. She sustained us through the hamburger years, our first home in Blooming Prairie, Minnesota, and our first garage. She was new, had brand-new grandparents, and received love from everyone. She was the original model for a mom and dad who were trying to work the bugs out. She wore real diapers with safety pins and had three-hour naps. She was the beginning. She is now a wife and the mother of our two grandchildren, Ryan and Anika. Tonya volunteers at her children's school in Alden,

Minnesota one day a week. The kindergarten and first grade classes receive a "Project Charlie" self esteem lesson every week. She is a Sunday-school teacher and 4-H leader, and she has pursued a career as a dental hygienist. She is a good friend to many. When Tonya was learning to walk, she encountered a few difficult days, because she was trying to incorporate my limp into her walk. She did that only for a few days before realizing she didn't have to walk like that. She is a wonderful example of a daughter. Her name means "beyond praise." Tonya and her husband, Bob, live and farm in Freeborn, Minnesota.

Our middle child, Aaron Nolan, drew a tough spot in the family, but he was stronger for it. Aaron arrived very quickly on a Sunday evening at 7:22 p.m. on September 7, 1975. We were at the hospital less than an hour before he was born, weighing seven pounds six and a half ounces and measuring twenty-one inches long. He cried less and had more patience than Tonya. He never in his life did anything first. But that made him special. He was the one we relaxed with. He helped us realize that a dog could kiss his face and he wouldn't get sick. He helped us understand that the world wouldn't collapse if he wet the bed or got his feet dirty. He was the child of busy, ambitious years and our first new home in the country. His thoughts about our home in the country were, "I'm stuck in the country without a farm." We lived on three acres, but not on a farm, and to him that meant being stuck. Without him, we never could have survived the job changes and the tedium and routine of marriage. He is now a husband and the father of four children, Cody, Emma, Cole, and Cade. He is a farmer and a local business owner. He and his wife, Jessie, live on a farm near Blooming Prairie, Minnesota. Jessie and I worked together for the last ten and a half years of my dental career; she is a dental hygienist. In her spare time, she is active with the school's PTO, softball coach for Emma's 6th grade softball team, and busy with 4-H. Aaron's name means "noble one."

Our third child, Lianna Maria, was usually a joy. She arrived after we spent a busy Monday morning getting a blue ribbon for cookies at the Mower County fair. It was Tonya's first year to enter a 4-H fair project in the fair in Austin, Minnesota. We had baked chocolate-chip cookies on Sunday to enter for judging. I knew when I woke that morning that a baby was going to be born. But the first order of business for the day was getting those cookies to the fair to be judged, so off we went. I sat in the car while Nolan, Tonya, and Aaron went to get the cookies judged. Aaron kept coming back to the car to check on me, and then he'd report back to Nolan. With the blue ribbon in hand, we called friends and deposited the children with them. Lianna Marie arrived on August 10, 1981, at 6:35 p.m., weighing seven pounds three ounces and measuring nineteen and a half inches long. (See - I had just enough time to get the cookies judged before she was born.) She readily accepted the milk-stained bibs, the hand-me-down clothes, and the business of our family. She was the one who got our leftover time in the years we took care of my mother. We thank her for surviving. She was the one who held on to us so tightly. Her name means "one who clings," and she did just that. She was the link to our past, and a reason for tomorrow. Though our hair changes color and she towers over us, she will always be our baby. She also pursued a career as a dental assistant, and she works in oral surgery. She spends her extra time serving on the board of our local Boys & Girls Club. She helps the Blooming Prairie Chamber of Commerce with the July 4th activities and teaches Sunday school. She and her husband, Travis, live on a farm near Waltham, Minnesota, and raise nursery pigs. They blessed us with two grandchildren, Addison and Aden.

Linda L. Christianson

I was now a busy mother with three young children, a dental career, and an interior-decorating business called Nolan's Interior that my husband and I ran together—and I was older. It was getting harder to keep up with things, but somehow I managed. All of our children were born in the summer—July, August, and September—and I was always grateful that I didn't have to walk on the slippery, snowy ground during those last months of pregnancy, when it was harder to get around. It was good to be pregnant during months when I had to simply stay cool and not worry about falling on the ice and snow. God had the right plan for my safety.

Because of my limp, my children were definitely rocked for the nine months before their births. That must be why they loved being rocked to sleep every night. Or was it simply that I loved that time with them, rocking them to sleep each and every night? Whatever it was, it was my special time with each one of them. I loved the hours in the middle of the night when they would wake to be fed and the house would be totally quiet. It was just that new baby and me, with no hectic distractions. I never hurried that time and enjoyed reading and watching each little baby in my arms. No matter how busy I was, I never gave that time up.

Camp Courage

Camp Courage is a permanent camp facility that is located on 305 acres of woodland. It is west of Maple Lake, Minnesota. Camp Courage opened in 1955 and was dedicated on July 8, 1956. This was a camp for crippled children and adults. The adjoining speech and hearing camp was completed in 1966 and dedicated by Vice-President Hubert H. Humphrey on August 14, 1966. The first year Camp Courage opened it had 300 campers. Campers had a safe place to challenge themselves with activities to help them develop life and leadership skills. I know I gained self-esteem, responsibility, the feeling of control in my life and of being valued by others. I recently made a visit to the camp and found after 30 years that a few structural changes had taken place. In 1994 they started replacing the six cabins for the campers lodging. By 1998 five new camper cabins had been finished. They omitted one of the boys' cabins. As I walked around the grounds and spoke with several young counselors, I thought, "it hasn't changed at all". Some of them had been campers in the past as I was. The counselors had the same determination to make the life of the camper *improved*. They were getting ready for the new children to arrive for "literacy" camp at 2:00 p.m. that day. Camp Courage was a significant part of my formative years. I spent two weeks of every summer at camp, a time period that was sandwiched before the surgery and recovery and going back to school. Camp Courage is a camp for physically handicapped children as well as speech- and hearing-impaired children. I made so many friends through counselors and with campers. My very best friend for many years was Mary Jo Kwako, from Detroit Lakes, Minnesota. I had traveled to her family's home and enjoyed her sister and brother as much as her. She was one year older than me, but we loved each other and couldn't wait for our two weeks together. We were always bunk partners and did everything together. She also had had polio and walked with crutches, while I had only braces. Mary Jo had contracted polio when she was ten years old, and she was very angry about her situation. I always felt that I was better off; I could get around without using crutches—or sticks, as they were sometimes called—and she couldn't.

We both had the opportunity to work at the camp when we became old enough. She was the secretary, and I was the camp director's daycare provider. I spent my entire day with a darling little boy named Tad. We became great pals, and we got to join in any event we wanted to, with whatever cabin we wanted to tag along with. We were always welcome. I was in my junior summer, and Mary Jo was in her senior summer. We had a fabulous time. It was a sad day when we both had to go back home and continue with our educations, knowing that we might not get the chance to spend such quality time together again. But we did! The next summer, I was an assistant to the kitchen crew and pitched in wherever they needed help. This was a little more physical, but I could make it work. I also spent time helping in crafts, in the office, and in the laundry. I did whatever I could just so I had a job for the summer. I didn't care what the job was; I just wanted to be there.

In the fall of 1966 I went off to Brainerd Area Vocational College for dental assisting, and Mary Jo was in her second year of college, studying to become a doctor. Her chance to become a doctor came to an end when she was killed in an automobile accident in the fall of 1967. She fell asleep at the wheel on her way home from college on a Friday night. I got the call from a friend who heard of the accident on the radio and called me. I was devastated. It was hard to believe that this bright, intelligent, loving person was gone at such a young age. She was just getting started. It didn't seem possible. But it was true. I went to her services and simply couldn't imagine life without her. But I did go on; I moved forward, as we all have to.

Those two working summers taught me so much. I had been a camper many summers for two weeks each year and numerous hospital stays were the only time I was away from my family. I was really home sick during those working summers, we only had a break to go home every other weekend but the friends I made and the experiences I had were worth it. Camp Courage taught me that courage is not the absence of fear. Rather, it is doing what it takes despite one's fear. Many times in my life, I have been afraid, and courage has gotten me through. I have many warmhearted memories of Camp Courage and my friend Mary Jo.

The present Camp Director, Tom Fogarty, was a camper at the speech and hearing camp in 1966. As we visited he said he remembered me working in the craft building that summer. He first came to work at the camp during the Vietnam War when it was hard to find male counselors. He has been there ever since. His wife, Mimi, is the current program manager. In 2005 Camp Courage had a big celebration celebrating its' 50 years. Other additions to the grounds were the gym added to the King recreation center (swimming pool) that was built in 1967. A new reception center was built in 1975 following a fire to the one I enjoyed while at camp that had been destroyed by fire in 1974. I know the children and adults that spend time there this summer will make memories just as I did all those years ago.

History of Mayo Clinic

Mayo Clinic is located forty-five miles from our home, and we are so fortunate to have it within driving distance. It was started on October 8, 1919, when the Mayo brothers and their wives, William and Hattie Mayo and Charles and Edith Mayo, signed a deed, to create Mayo Clinic. At first it had six partners, each with their own expertise. "I look through a half opened door; into the future full of interest; intriguing beyond my power to describe," wrote Dr. William Mayo in 1931. He had no idea what he was creating.

Dr. William Mayo and Hattie had two daughters, Carrie and Phoebe, both of whom married prominent Mayo Clinic surgeons. Hattie studied architecture at Carleton College in Northfield. They also had three children who died in infancy.

Dr. Charles Mayo and Edith had six children, as well as two who died in infancy. They also adopted a daughter and served as foster parents to a son. Edith was the first trained nurse in Rochester and served as Mayo's anesthetist, office nurse, and bookkeeper before she married Charles.

The Mayo Historical Suite is located in the Plummer Building. We are so fortunate to have this facility within forty-five miles of us. Because so many trips were necessary, proximity eased the burden.

History of Gillette State Hospital for Crippled Children

Jessie Haskins influenced the mission of Gillette State Hospital. In 1895 she was a student at Carleton College in Northfield, Minnesota. She had developed a deformity of the spine early in her life and felt that the state should help provide care for others with illness and deformities. In 1896 she was invited to speak at the Fifth Minnesota State Conference in Red Wing, Minnesota. Following the conference she met Dr. Arthur Gillette. This meeting took place before the legislative session in January 1897. She wanted to discuss with Dr. Gillette if he would be interested in a state institution for crippled and deformed children. When Gillette was young, his father thought he should stay on the farm to work, but his mother had different ideas. He attended Hamline University and continued his education with an internship at St. Joseph's Hospital in St. Paul. In 1886 he went to New York City to study orthopedic medicine and was a house surgeon at the New York Orthopedic Dispensary and Hospital. After returning to Minnesota, he opened a general medical practice in the Seven Corners area of St. Paul and provided free care to many patients. The state was still working to find a place for the state hospital. On April 23, 1897, the bill to establish a "Minnesota Institute for Crippled and Deformed

Children" was introduced and passed. The first patient at Gillette Hospital was from Pine City, Minnesota.

My parents had talked with social services at St. Mary's Hospital in Rochester and it was decided that I could transfer my care to Gillette Children's Hospital in St. Paul. Minnesota. My first medical evaluation appointment was on January 19, 1962. Since October 1, 1948, my medical and orthopedic care had been performed at St. Mary's Hospital in Rochester. My father would make arrangements with the local bank, Farmers and Merchants State Bank of Blooming Prairie, Minnesota and pre-payment would be made for my up coming surgery. This went on for years. At one point my father said that mom just made a payment every month to Mayo Clinic. He also told me that the bill from Mayo came one month marked "Paid in full" and he never was sure how that Mayo bill was paid. Did someone pay it or was it just forgiven? My parents told me that I was finally paid for when I was married. At that first appointment at Gillette it was decided that I would return for the next summer's surgery. I was admitted on July 3, 1962, and had left-ankle arthrodesis surgery on July 6, 1962. This was the surgery that enabled me to finally get rid of my last brace. I was a patient until July 27, 1962. This was the only orthopedic surgery I had performed there. It was the longest month of my life. Our ward was large, filled with lots of girls my age. I missed a cousins wedding during my stay, we could only have visitors on Sundays and I was so lonesome. I remember one of the girls in that ward had an amazing voice and sang "Oh Holy Night" to us at bedtime every night. I did not keep in touch with any of my hospital friends. I think I simply wanted to forget about the entire experience. My parents were not able to make the drive because my mother worked on Sundays. She wasn't able to get off work to visit me during that two-hour visiting time from 2:00 to 4:00 pm on Sundays only. I wrote a letter to her boss asking for him to let her have time off to come and visit for one Sunday and then she was able to make a visit. My parents had friends living in St. Paul and they were able to visit on some of the Sundays. My follow-up care was monitored for a short time, and my last examination was on August 23, 1966. I was approaching the age of twenty-one and would no longer be eligible to receive care. I returned to Mayo Clinic in Rochester, Minnesota to continue my orthopedic care.

In 1977 the Gillette Children's Hospital became part of the St. Paul-Ramsey Medical Center and the Ramsey Clinic. It is now called the Ramsey Hospital Campus. Gillette Children's Hospital is no longer a state hospital.

The Minnesota Twins have a designated day for children from Gillette Children's Hospital to come to Target Field in down town Minneapolis, Minnesota to enjoy a baseball game in the new outdoor stadium.

Disadvantages and Advantages of living with physical limitations

Certain things make my life easier, and I generally try to take advantage of them when I can. A vacation can be challenging for me. For example, I have to travel with my folding crutches so I will have them to be able to get around when I take my left leg brace off. If I travel with a large suitcase they will fold and fit inside and become checked luggage. If I travel with only carry on luggage they become a necessary medical needs item and travel as extra carry on luggage uncounted. These folding crutches fit nicely in a lawn chair bag and are easy to carry. Traveling by plane is time consuming because it takes a long time to get through security. I always have to arrive at the airport very early. It can take up to forty-five minutes for me to get through security. When traveling with my dental office to California for a dental association meeting I was escorted to a family bathroom by two female security guards at the airport. A co-worker from the office was asked to follow the two security guards and myself and to carry my entire carry-on luggage. I had to take my brace off so they could examine the inside of it and pat down my leg to make sure I didn't have any substances packed inside that brace. Fortunately we had arrived in plenty of time. I had warned them that it might take a while to get through security. That was the only time I have ever had to take my brace off. Usually I warn the guards as I am about to pass through the scanner that I will set off all the bells and whistles, and as soon as I pass through, I am asked to step aside. The full check takes another ten minutes, and then I'm on my way. It is difficult for me to walk with my shoes off so it is just a bit of a challenge to do all this and board the plane in time for takeoff. I love to travel but am leaning toward ground travel. It is important to me to be able to take care of all my needs by myself as much as possible. I know the day is coming when I will have to accept help. When help is offered I try to accept it willingly and thankfully.

Since I had to go back to wearing a full leg brace on my left leg in 1984, I have worn dresses only on very special occasions, perhaps for a wedding or something at church. I always wear long dresses to cover my brace, but that is often not the current style. With the really short dresses in style now (that will change next year), I just avoid wearing dresses. Otherwise, I always wear pants of some sort. I miss wearing dresses, and it is more special to dress up in a fancy dress. I cannot wear fancy shoes, so slacks or jeans are the best option for me.

The next disadvantage is that I am forever putting holes in my pants. The brace has leather protectors over the hinges on both sides, but if I bump into anything hard, it may make a hole. If I sit on something hard, the back of my brace will make a hole in the back of my pant leg. Even walking normally is problematic; the rubbing on the inside of my pants will eventually make a hole from wear. During Minnesota winters, if I slip on the ice and snow, I will probably have a hole in my pants from where the hinge hits the ground. Sometimes it is hard shopping for slacks because during the summer Capri pants are the style and not full-length slacks. It is a good thing that I enjoy sewing, because I am more than capable of repairing almost anything that needs my attention.

The braces are expensive and I need time to have them cleaned, adjusted when needed and hot to wear in the summer. I am fortunate that I can go to Rochester for any adjustments and repair. The fact that I have two is necessary so if one were to need repair and I couldn't wear it, I would still be able to get around with the aid of the other. During the summer months they are hot and I only wear slacks. If it is really a warm day I might be found with the brace off and sitting in a lawn chair reading a book under a shade tree or tubing down the Root River.

The advantages of having a physical limitation help make my life easier. It is very helpful to be able to use my handicap parking. On nice days, when the weather is great, I like the extra walking, but when the weather is hazardous, I definitely use the handicap parking. Usually my friends are more than happy to take me along on errands, and then we all can use my parking privilege. Sometimes I joke that the only reason they ask me along is that they want to use my handicap parking. It comes in handy at the airport and when traveling.

I usually don't have to wait in any lines at places like Disney. Someone always notices me quickly and helps us get to the head of the line so I don't have to stand very long. By using a cane on a regular basis, I have gained some respect. People are usually very courteous to me. I am finding that young people, though they are generally in a hurry, will pause and open a door for me if we are walking toward the same entrance. I always thank them and say, "Go ahead—I'm not in a hurry". Some say, "Go ahead, I need to slow down and not be in such a hurry". Children are very curious and courteous. When I am at our local school, listening to children read in my grandchildren's classes, or attending a grandchild's program the kids are always so polite. They would help me with getting me a chair and holding the doors, and I never hear the question "What happened to you?" They see me there a lot, so perhaps they've stopped noticing that I get around a little differently. Such innocence they have.

It was a great opportunity for me to attend a Triennial Convention for my church in St. Louis in 2001 as a delegate with disabilities. It was a fabulous excuse to take a trip with my best friend, Barb, who helped me in grade school when I arrived with crutches and again in high school when I had surgery. We stayed in a very nice hotel with all the other delegates and were treated especially well. On that journey, we had the opportunity to visit the Gateway Arch. Barb had to work so hard to get me down the long, steep walkway to the Arch and then again to get me up and out of the area. It was beautiful to see, and I am so glad we were able to do it. Now, all these years later, I know I would not be able to make that journey. Now is the time for me to pick and choose what I want to do. Sometimes it is just too difficult, and I have to say, "Not this time."

In 2001 I was able to be part of a research study to test a new brace hinge. Some long leg brace hinges are locked for support and some are free motion. This test was completed in the motion-analysis laboratory at Mayo Clinic. My left leg was fitted with a long leg brace, similar to the one I have worn since I was thirty-six. It had a lock hinge that would unlock, as I needed. If I reached down and slid the hinges up the brace, the brace could bend. It was very difficult for me to use, because I was driving a standard-transmission car and needed to use my left leg to operate the clutch. I had to wear my regular brace to drive my car. It also didn't work when I wanted to ride my bike, because it didn't bend when I needed it to. However, I did wear the brace as much as possible and completed the test. It was bulkier than my usual one, so I had to wear large pants to accommodate the size of the hinge. It did fit under my work scrubs, but it was inconvenient to have to adjust the hinge every time I sat down. The hinge was designed to release when the weight came off the leg and lock when I put weight down. When the test was over, they removed the lock hinge and replaced it with one that would be suitable for my needs. It was very interesting to walk in the motion lab with cameras all around the room. I walked back and forth so they could compile the information they needed as I passed over a marked area in the floor. This marked area was a metal square that had holes in it and a camera was under it to compile information. I asked how many people were in the test, what their ages were, and why they needed to wear a brace. Almost all of them were polio survivors, and some were stroke victims. The youngest child in the study was eight years old. He had contracted the poliovirus from his childhood vaccine.

Obtaining a driver's license was a very interesting event. My grandmother, who lived on our farm, had a small automatic transmission car. My father thought it would be much easier for me to navigate the test with her smaller car. I made the appointment and completed the behind-the-wheel test. When we got back to the office, the examiner handed me my temporary driver's license with "restricted to automatic transmission" stamped on it. I was so surprised and disappointed. My family's car was a very long Dodge Dart with standard transmission. I had learned to operate a standard transmission by driving our old pickup out in the field, over the furrows, bouncing all over the place—and now I couldn't drive it. They had to be kidding. Both of my family's vehicles were standard transmission, and now the only car I could drive was my grandmother's. I looked at the examiner and asked if he had an appointment time available that afternoon, and he looked at his appointment book and said he did. I suggested that he let me have that appointment time and that I would be back to retake the behind-the-wheel examination. I showed up with that big car, all set to retake the test, and I passed, just as I knew I would. The restriction was lifted. I did understand that the examiner had done the right thing, but I simply wasn't willing to have that "restricted" stamp on my license. This is a good example of how my parents never stopped me from doing what I wanted to do. They could have said that I had my license and that I should be happy with that. But they knew this wasn't good enough for me. I wanted and deserved to have a license just like everyone else's. I simply had to prove that I was capable of handling the car safely.

Bullying has become a general concern among young people. It is on the news almost daily. Recently, an article in our church magazine, which I shared with the women's group at my church, mentioned that we should be aware of the problem. When we see children or adults showing disrespect to another person, it is all right to step in and help. When I look back on a situation I encountered in seventh or eighth grade, I see now that I was a victim of bullying. At the time, I never thought about what was happening as bullying; now I see it definitely was. It happened like this. *Gun Smoke* was a popular show on television, and my family used to listen to it on the radio since we didn't have a television. We formed a line around the room, and I usually sat with a doll on my lap. The boys in my class thought my new name should be "Chester", after a character on that show who walked with a limp from an injury. I had just moved back to this area after living for a short time in Pine City, Minnesota. I'd been away from fourth grade to sixth grade, and during that time the O'Leary country (rural) school had been consolidated into the Blooming Prairie school district. I was still adjusting and trying to fit in. After only a few days of being called "Chester", I decided that I didn't want to spend the next five years with this nickname. I went into the office one day and asked to talk to the school principal. I explained my situation. I had not discussed this with my parents at all. I knew I had to make things better for myself at school. I had enough challenges to deal with already, and this wasn't going to be one of them. Soon after that day, the physical-education teacher gathered all the boys in my class and held a lecture of some sort in the gym. He probably explained that I had requested to not be called "Chester" anymore. I think he handled the situation perfectly, because from that day forward, the name "Chester" never came my way again. I don't remember my parents ever bringing it up, either. I am sure the school called them and explained the situation, but they let me handle my own circumstances and didn't stop me from taking care of it the way I felt was best.

Shortly after that, I got a new nickname: "Bergie", created from Bergstrom, my last name at the time. I was one of ten Linda's in my class, and we all went by different names so we could be kept apart in conversation. To this day, I have many close friends who call me "Bergie", and I love it. My children, when they were small didn't care for the name, and they would correct my friends when they were visiting, saying, "Her name isn't "Bergie"—it's Linda." But "Bergie" has stuck and it's a good fit, and I'll continue to wear the name. A few past co-workers have tagged me "LC," for Linda Christianson, and I answer to that as well. On an occasion I'll hear "Pooch" sent my way. All of these nicknames are better than "Chester".

Riding My Bike

One thing I have enjoyed since I was a small child is riding my
bicycle. One joyous summer evening, I came out of the barn after
milking the cows and found a beautiful green bike waiting. The best
part was that my parents had bought it especially for me. My birthday
wasn't in the summer, so I'd gotten a new bike for no reason. I think
I was about eight years old, and I was so excited. This was something
way beyond my capabilities, I thought—but I thought this way for only
a short time. My dad said to straddle the chain guard; sit on the seat
with both legs out to the sides, and just coast down the hill. I was not
to worry about falling; I should just concentrate on steering and try to
make it to the bottom of the hill. I'm sure I tipped over many times
and hurt my knees, but I don't remember that part. I do remember the
excitement of the entire family as they cheered me down that hill.

Each night after milking, my dad would come out and find me waiting
and ready for the next lesson. He helped me onto the seat, and again
I had to let my legs hang out of the way and coast down the hill. My
grandmother's house was just around the corner at the bottom of that
small hill. I advanced to going around the corner and stopping however I
could on the grass without getting hurt. What a thrill. Once my balance
was good, I didn't get hurt from tipping over on the grass, and I could

stop with my own two feet, I was allowed to pedal and stop anywhere I wanted to. We lived on a gravel road, and riding on this was much more difficult than riding on the hard-packed driveway and yard, but I gave it all I had, and I was on my way.

We loved it when the road grader came along and made a really smooth edge along the side of the road. Patty and I would bike all the way to the corner and back many times until the first rain came along, melting the edge right into the rest of the gravel road. We would ride our bikes to the O'Leary country (rural) school, picking up kids along the way, and I made it all the way to school and back home. Our family's farm was the farthest to the east, and we would pick up families as we made our way to school.

My bicycle days are not over yet. I had a child carrier on the back of my bike when my children were young, and every one of them enjoyed lots of rides with me. We lived in our little village, and every night Nolan and I would each have someone or something in our child carriers. I usually had our pet, a small gray poodle, and he had Tonya. When Aaron was little he rode in my carrier, and the dog moved to the basket. By the time Lianna was born Tonya and Aaron could ride their own bikes. When the next generation came along, my grandchildren all took rides around town in my child carrier. When Cole, one of my grandsons, set out for his first ride with Grandma, he cried as the helmet went on. He cried as we went down the driveway. He cried as we rode by the utility men working on our block, and they said, "He doesn't seem to like that so much." I replied, "He doesn't know he's going to like this yet." By the time we returned home, he was no longer crying—in fact, he was enjoying the ride. Cole is also the grandchild who copied my walk. When we were taking care of the kids one day, I started walking to the kitchen, and Nolan said that Cole watched me intently and then took steps that copied mine. He did it only a few times, but he was walking with a limp like mine.

Our youngest grandson, Aden, didn't get as many rides as the others, because I was approaching a time when I didn't feel safe riding with children anymore. I didn't want to harm any child in that carrier. However, he enjoys his rides in my latest addition—a beautiful blue Meridian Schwinn tricycle. It has a fabulous basket that he can ride in. Perhaps this summer Aden will learn to ride a bike by himself and we can ride together.

Biking is the only thing I do that can be called exercise besides just walking and getting myself around. One day I went bike shopping and Nolan said, "You better take the pickup in case you find a bike that will work for you." I was having a difficult time getting my right leg over the bar because it was too high. If I got on, I couldn't get off without a step to stand on, which was not safe. I took his suggestion and left with the pickup. It was a good thing I did, because I needed to put that new tricycle in it to get home. I bought it at Fleet Farm. To test it out, I rode the bike carefully around the store, stopping at the intersections, letting people go by, and visiting with other shoppers. A store employee approached me and said "You can't ride that bike in the store." I explained that I couldn't find a bike I could ride anymore and that this one seemed to be fitting my needs. For the amount of money I was about to spend, I had to be sure it was right for me before making the purchase. She simply asked me to be very careful, and I assured her I would and continued my journey around the store.

The bike did come home with me. I am looking forward to spring days when I can again feel safe doing my errands around town, get some exercise, and enjoy time with my grandchildren. My grandchildren love my new bike. When they ask permission, they can ride it. The kids in town stop when I come down the street; they give me thumbs up sign and say, "That's a really cool bike." The older people ask, "Where did you get that bike?" I can get on and off with ease. I feel safe, and I get all the exercise I want in my little village, going everywhere I need to go.

End Polio Now

I didn't choose polio; I didn't choose the crutches, cane, and braces; I chose to thrive. I have never known any other way of getting around, so it must be that I have simply adjusted. I firmly believe that being happy is an attitude. You can make physical changes to help improve a situation, but if your attitude is negative, it is all just window dressing. I am and will continue to be a survivor. Whatever handicap polio left me with; polio has not claimed my life or my heart. I will continue to pray each and every day for patience to plan my day by prioritizing my needs and to be very persistent. Knowing the limits of what I can do is the most important thing of all. This, by far, is the hardest thing I have had to adjust to.

My thanks go out to Rotary International (www.rotary.org) for all they are doing to end polio. In 1985, Rotary vowed to stop polio. Since 1988, Rotary International and its partners in the Global Polio Eradication Initiative (GPEI), the World Health Organization (WHO), Unicef, and the US Centers for Disease Control and Prevention (CDC) have worked to wipe polio from the face of the earth. Rotary is a volunteer service organization of 1.2 million men and women. Rotary began immunizing children against polio in 1985 and became a leader in the effort. Rotary's main responsibilities are fundraising, advocacy, and volunteer recruitment. To date, Rotary has contributed more than $900 million to the polio-eradication effort. There are 33,000 clubs in 150 countries, with a million members spread across numerous geographical areas. Rotary is able to reach out to governments worldwide. Thanks to Rotary and its partners, the world has seen polio cases plummet by more than 99 percent, preventing five million instances of childhood paralysis and 250,000 deaths. When Rotary began its eradication work, polio infected more than 350,000 children annually. In 2009, fewer than 1,700 cases were reported. The final cases represent the final one percent and are the most difficult and expensive to prevent. That's why it is so important to generate the funding needed, as the Rotary slogan says, to "End Polio Now." The bottom line is this: as long as polio threatens even one child anywhere in the world, all children—wherever they live—remain at risk. On Thursday, February 23, 2012, KTTC Rochester broadcast that lights that said "END POLIO NOW" were shining on the outside of the Mayo Siebens Building until 10:00 p.m. that evening. The Rochester Rotary Club sponsored this. The slogan for Rotary is "We are this close"—to ending polio, to changing the world. "If we all have the fortitude to see this effort through to the end then we will eradicate polio," said Bill Gates, co-chair of the Bill and Melinda Gates Foundation.

Immunizations are still needed in four countries: Nigeria, Pakistan, Afghanistan, and India. In 2010, India reported forty-two cases; in 2011, only one case was reported. India's Rotary had a polio immunization day, and 70 percent of the country was vaccinated. They sent 125 volunteers to complete this project, at a cost of nearly $50 billion. Each dose costs just ten cents. Uttar Pradesh is overpopulated and has poor sanitation. Twice a year, children are treated in Pardesh. They start with 17 million children, and after six days of vaccinations 136 million children had been treated. If we don't get every case, polio will be back—stronger than ever. It's just a plane ride away.

For many people, polio is part of the distant past. Some people have never heard of polio. I went to meet Peg Kehret at the public library in Austin, Minnesota, for the signing of her book, *My First Steps: The Year I Got Polio.* She is a children's book author targeting twelve-year-old readers. The room was full of children of that age and their parents. This was the first time I met Peg Kehret, though we had corresponded by mail. When I approached the table to have her sign my book, I introduced myself. She got up, came around the table, and gave me a big hug. What a treat to meet her and receive such a warm welcome. As I was leaving, a mother stopped me. She and her daughter asked me a lot of questions about polio. Neither one of them had ever heard of it before that night. Ginny (Goldberg) Baynes, Peg Kehret, millions of others and me live it as a daily reality. We all need to help the Rotary with the task they have set out to complete.

I was asked to speak at the monthly Rotary meeting in Owatonna, Minnesota, where my sister, Lonna, is a member. I took time off work to attend. After dinner, I was named a Paul Harris Fellow in appreciation of tangible and significant assistance given for the furtherance of better understanding and friendly relations among people of the world. It is a tribute to a person whose life demonstrates the Rotary Foundation's way and purpose. My sister said it was my recognition for my years with polio and the courage I put forth to help others and myself. It is simply the way I do things every day, because I know no other way. Remember, I think I am "normal."

Paul Harris founded Rotary in 1905. He was brought to live with his grandparents at a young age, and they raised him. While Paul was away at college at Princeton, his grandfather, Howard Harris, passed away. Howard had given Paul a road map for success and had taught him to strive for one thing above all else: tolerance. Paul finished studying law at the University of Iowa and after traveling for five years; he began to practice in Chicago, Illinois. Paul Harris was the first president of the newly formed National Association of Rotary Clubs in Chicago, which encompassed sixteen clubs. He continued inspiring Rotary clubs until his death in 1947. Today there are nearly a million members. We should be grateful for the work Rotary does. I know that millions of other parents and I are.

My Last Steps

In April of 1995, I attended the Minnesota Dental Convention in St. Paul, Minnesota. I had the opportunity to hear Rabbi Kurshner speak just after Timothy McVeigh bombed the Alfred P. Murrah Federal Building in downtown Oklahoma City, killing two hundred innocent adults and children. The site is now a beautiful memorial and museum. I have visited the memorial, and it is breathtaking. Rabbi Kurshner made strong points about the way we should live our lives. I am reminded daily of these, as I have them posted on my bulletin board in my sewing room. They are as follows:

1. "Share with others." Human life must be shared. When human souls connect, love is formed. Sharing life with others lets us know we are loved. It lets us know we are important. Make sure you have someone's hand to hold along life's journey.

2. "If you want to feel good about your life, you have to be ready to accept pain as part of living." This can be physical pain and distress, as well as pain that others cause you.

3. "If life is lived right, it hurts." We have to be brave enough to chance feeling. If you don't feel pain, you are not really living your

life to the fullest. We will all lose someone we love, and loving is the appropriate thing to do, but the emptiness can hurt.

4. "It is important to have made a difference in this world." I always wanted my children to remember to do something nice for someone every day. The best way we can make a difference in this world is to love one another. It is important to leave something behind that will go on after we are no longer here. Perhaps you can plant a tree, have a child, or write a book, the Rabbi suggests. At this time in my life, I have completed all three. Now I pray that my children and grandchildren will make a difference in this world. My life itself is my final reward for all I have accomplished.

Romans 8:28 says, "He does have a purpose for me in my difficulties and we know that all things work together for good to them that love God, to them who are called according to his purpose. He doesn't take away the pain and suffering that come with living in the world, but his strong and tender hands never cease to hold me tight."

My final steps are getting slower, making my days longer; I need a lot more of the patience I try to carry with me. Symptoms that are probably post-polio syndrome (PPS) are with me every day. A medical physician has not diagnosed me with PPS, but I definitely fit the criteria. The patient must have a recorded diagnosis of having had polio. For me, sixty-three and a half years of records from Mayo Clinic show that I have had polio. Next, the patient must have had improvement from onset. Being able to go from braces on both legs to finally getting that last brace off at age sixteen was a gratifying experience. The next step is that the patient must have had one to two decades of stability. Those were the years during which I married my wonderful helpmate and had my children. Those years, for me, were from age sixteen to age thirty-six, the years during which I lived without braces of any kind. Finally, the patient must present with new symptoms that are related to polio and have not been diagnosed as some other illness. When Lianna was three, I had to go back to wearing a long leg brace on my left leg. The criteria had been met.

PPS appears fifteen to fifty years after the onset of polio. It is an illness of the nervous system and causes weakness, fatigue, and muscle and joint pain. It progresses slowly. It doesn't spread, but the muscles that regained some strength now show nerve damage. The nerves break down over time and lead to weakened muscles again. It shows up very slowly. I always joke that I am so glad aging happens slowly so I can get used to it along the way. The treatment for PPS is to stay as active as possible in spite of the weakening muscles. It is important to get lots of exercise and rest and to find the right balance. It may be necessary to use ice, heat, or physical therapies like massage to help relieve the pain. Chiropractic care can result in more endurance. A healthy lifestyle will promote optimum functioning in all levels of our lives: physical, mental, social, and spiritual. Maintaining a comfortable weight can reduce stress on the joints. It may also be necessary to use assistive devices, such as a cane, to make activities easier. I now use my cane on a regular basis. I use my crutches when my brace is off. I strive to maintain my constructive attitude, because depression is very common; I feel that I generally have rational control of my emotions.

It is an early morning in springtime. Spring brings new beginnings. In Minnesota this year, spring sprang up before we set the clocks ahead for daylight savings time. Spring brings freshness and new life to the earth. It encourages me to go forward with this day as the first day of the rest of my life. While camping last summer, I ran across a saying on a wall plaque in an antique shop that said, "I can't promise I'll be with you for the rest of your life, but I can promise I'll love you for the rest of mine." Where will my steps lead me in my journey? So far, they have led me down all the right paths, and I promise to love all the people in my life for the rest of my life. As the Rabbi said, it is important to have made a difference in this world, and I have tried to make that difference.

We live in a small farming community in southern Minnesota. You know you live in a small town when pickups outnumber cars on the main street. You get a get-well card after you miss church on Sunday. You call the wrong number and wind up talking for half an hour. Someone asks how you are and really listens to what you have to say. The New Year's baby is born on February 1. It was a wonderful community to raise our children. They enjoyed attending elementary and high school; they were nurtured at a small rural Church, Red Oak Grove Lutheran. They have all grown up to be respectable adults and live in small communities where they are active and supportive and will make a difference in their community.

Children's and Husband's Responses

In order to give a good picture of my family, I asked each of my children the same question I previously asked my siblings: What do you remember about growing up with a mom with polio? Here are their responses.

Response from Tonya:

As a child, I don't think I knew any differently. You could do everything everyone else did, as far as I knew. You went to work like all parents. You had a family and worked hard at home. We had a large garden, and you would sit on your butt to weed and pick green beans for hours in the evening and then come in to can. You hung clothes on the line every day and used a red wagon to get them to the clothesline and back. Our home was always spic and span.

I remember not liking when other kids stared at you. I knew you were different, and I didn't want anyone else to notice. They didn't know the person you were; they saw only the physical differences. I'm not sure if making me sew things over and over and over had anything to do with polio or if it was just you being a perfectionist. At the time, it was horrible, but I know now that you don't do things just to do them, you do things in the approved manner. When you had to get your new brace at age thirty-six, it was a defeat for you. We all just wanted you to walk without pain. Your ankles fused and hip replaced—it was heartbreaking for us to see and not fair that you had to go through so much. I did not like seeing you in pain.

I remember having a lot of responsibility at a very early age, but I'm not sure if that was polio-related or just the economic situation for our family at the time. I was just responsible. (Author's note: My sister Lonna, also a firstborn, had this same feeling.) I was focused on helping you out. You never talked much about your journey with polio, so we maybe didn't know what we were expected to think. I do remember a conversation about you being chosen, that Dad chose you despite your disability. It didn't happen after you were married. When a couple experiences a tragedy in their marriage that leaves a spouse disabled, it is a different story. Dad chose you as you were. I think of that so often.

As an adult, looking at you, I am so proud of you. You have taught us to give and give. To work hard and never give up. To do the things we enjoy and help others along the way. You are so talented and can do anything. Your talents are so much more than so many others'. Your limitations have *never* really been limitations but more of a challenge. I think if someone told you "No," you would think, "Oh, yeah? Watch me." Our pastor recently gave a sermon about what the dash in between your birth and death dates means. Your dash is amazing.

Quotes from Tonya's children:

I asked Ryan and Anika what their thoughts were when I said "Grandma."

Ryan (age eleven): "She can fix anything" and "Grandma helps a lot of other people."

Anika (age nine): "Grandma makes really pretty hand-stamped cards. She is really good at pegs and jokers, and she *always* has chocolate-chip cookies."

Good luck with this project. I can't wait to read it.

Love you so much, Tonya

Response from Aaron:

You were a great mom. You were always doing for others. The thing I liked the most is that you let me be me. Our home always had something going on. It was hard for me to see you struggle with your disease, and I always wondered what it would be like if you didn't have it. I realize now that it made you who you are, and probably made me who I am. I can't imagine the battle you have gone through. You won the battle well. (Author's note: Aaron liked to go to Arkansas with a friend, and he generally liked to bring back a coonhound. On one particular trip, I said, "No more dogs." After he returned, it took me only five days to discover that a new pup was hidden at his grandpa's. Yes, he got to keep the pup.)

These are quotes from Aaron's children:

Cade (age eight): "My grandma likes to play games with me, and I like her cookies." (Cade is really good at pegs and jokers.)

Cole (age ten): "I love to go camping with my grandma. She likes to ride bikes with me." (Author's note: Remember, he was the little one who didn't like his first bike ride in that child carrier.) "We play games, and she bakes us cookies."

Emma (age twelve): "My grandma is special to me because she does many things for me. She sews me things, and she goes for bike rides and makes my favorite cookies. I think my grandma is so strong since she has polio. We all enjoy hearing about her childhood and how she grew up with polio, but it makes us sad. We like to see her suitcase full of the braces and things from when she was a child. We love our grandma a lot. She may not be able to do the things other grandmas do, but she does not give up and always makes us feel special."

Love you and good luck, Aaron

Response from Lianna:

One word that comes to my mind is *courage*. It was not difficult to come up with appropriate words for each letter: Caring, Outgoing, Understanding, Receptive, Attractive, Genuine, Exciting to have in our lives. As a child, I had the privilege of having you invent, fix, and do just about anything. Support was always present. School, church, and community events were always so lucky to have you on board. Whatever the task was, it would be done perfectly if you were on the committee. I dreaded summers and fair projects since I had to do everything perfectly. To this day, I still ask of each of my projects, "Does it have to be fair-perfect?" As an adult, I value you more than ever. As a mom, you have always encouraged me and given me good advice when needed. My family and I are so extremely blessed to have such a perfect role model in our lives. Thank you for giving me the fundamentals that made me the person I am today.

These are quotes from Lianna's children:

When you asked me this question, I thought it was very important to get a response from my children separately.

Addison (age seven): "She is a superhero, because she can fix anything. My grandma is helpful, nice, awesome, kind and loving."

Aden (age five) "Grandma can fix socks with holes in them and she makes *awesome* choc-chip cookies"

I love you, Lianna

Response from Nolan:

Linda and I started our lives together in high school. Prom was the beginning of our relationship. Then she went off to college, and I finished high school. After a few years, we renewed our relationship. Linda was living in St. Paul with a dental assistant classmate, Lanita. A college friend, Warren, and I would go to St. Paul to visit Linda and Lanita. Just as our life together began on June 14, 1969, theirs did as well on August 9, 1969.

Our lives were hectic as we went about building a future. We started by buying our first fixer-upper home in Blooming Prairie, Minnesota. Our parents thought we were crazy. The house needed so much work, but I was able to fix anything. We spent hours after work each day making this house a home. Besides getting settled in, we were also soon-to-be new parents. We had no idea how this pregnancy would go, and it was not going to be easy for Linda to carry a baby, but she never complained. Getting Tonya to daycare and then going to work went just fine. As our family grew with the birth of our son, Aaron, so did our dream of building a larger home in the country. We worked and finished our new home while caring for two children.

The children began Sunday school, and, of course, Linda needed to be a teacher. Soon they began swimming lessons and T-ball, and we cared for a large yard and garden. The weeding, canning, kids, and house kept us very busy. At this time, Linda felt incomplete and decided we needed a third child. She was older now, and, because of her limitations, this pregnancy was going to be more strenuous. We had a business in Blooming Prairie called Nolan's Interior. Linda was working at the dental office and at the store, Nolan's Interior and managing the home. She did not make a complaint, however, and soon our daughter Lianna was born. The activities of a nine-year-old, six-year-old, and new baby were here to stay. Our lives showed no sign of slowing down.

There has never been a "can't do it" when it came to Linda's family, friends, or church. She never says no, claiming instead, "Busy people always have time to help out." To this day, you'll have a hard time finding her at home. She volunteers at the church all the time. If someone in the community needs something, even a meal for their family, she will be there. Her commitment to her family and friends is endless. She has a bucket list of things she wants to do, and she will do everything on her list. Following her hip replacement in 1996, we decided to move from our split foyer home with steps and a large yard to care for and to build our last home in Blooming Prairie, Minnesota. This home was built handicap accessible. All doorways in our home are wider and the entry made with no steps. Everything that Linda needs is on the main floor so she doesn't have to go to the basement except by her choice.

I wish you the best of luck with your project. You have wanted to complete this for a long time. Now was the right time.

Love, Nolan

How can I follow the words of my loving husband, children, and grandchildren? As Oprah says, "Everything you do and say shows the world who you really are. Let it be the truth." I did what I set out to do, raising my children to have respect for themselves and others. I can only be thankful for what they have become, and I will continue to live a life of gratitude. We must do all the good we can today, because tomorrow is not promised to us.

Closing

Thank you for taking the time to read my one and only book. This book is based solely on my emotions and feelings. I hope I have left you with inspiration and encouragement to accomplish the tasks awaiting you in your life, regardless of what limitations you may or may not have. You can do anything you want to do with a lot of prayer, faith, and trust. Live your life to the fullest. Be careful how you live. You may be the only Bible some people will ever read.

Linda

Epilogue

Ginny (Goldberg) Baynes lives in Portland, Oregon, with her husband, Mike. They enjoy traveling and taking care of Ursa, their dog. After Ginny received her medical records, she wanted to cry when she thought about how she had gone through so much. She also had many surgeries. She said, "I can't imagine how my parents dealt with all the health problems." I reminded her that we were so young that we don't remember that part of our lives. Ginny loves to spend time in her garden.

Peg Kehret now lives in Wilkeson, Washington, and continues to write books. Her love for animals is ever present. She mentioned that she did not have to be hospitalized for surgeries after her onset. Peg is experiencing some muscle weakness, pain, and fatigue but is still able to walk and does use a cane occasionally.

Special Thanks

Thank you to my parents, Arnold and the late Mildred Bergstrom, for never stopping me from pursuing my goals. They made sure that I was able to try anything I thought was achievable.

My immediate family has always been a great deal of assistance. Nolan has never stopped being there for me. My children understood that I needed their legs to help me with many of the projects I undertook and they willingly did what they could.

Much thanks to Annie Anderson, general manager of *The Times*, our county's weekly newspaper, for helping with the process of submitting the manuscript and photos. Her computer knowledge was crucial to completing this project. For her many hours I am forever grateful.

(bptimes@frontiernet.net or annieanderson1974@hotmail.com)

Tammy Wolf was inspirational in designing the cover for my book. She is a local photographer who does sports events at our school, wedding pictures, family portraits, and much more. (wolftammy@ymail.com)

The encouragement I needed to make my decision to retire came from Dr. Carol Holtz at the Austin Medical Center in Austin, Minnesota.

I thank her for her continued care and encouragement along my life's journey.

Thank you to Denise Walters at Gillette Hospital for editing my information from the book *We Hold This Treasure* by Steven E. Koop, MD. I did not know the history of Gillette Hospital. As of 1977, it is no longer a nonprofit hospital. I thank the doctors who completed the surgery that made it possible for me to be brace-free for twenty years.

Laura Calchera was eager to help me with permission to use quotes from the book *"Puppies for Sale"* by Dan Clark. (www.danclarkspeaker. com). Thank you for the help.

I obtained the Mayo Clinic information from many of their brochures, which are available to the millions of patients they see annually.

Two wonderful friends, Barb and Vikki, made it possible to continue the process of editing the rough drafts when I started writing this book. I value their friendship and encouraging words along my life's journey. They have always been there when I needed them most.

Much thanks to Rotary International for continued support to ending polio. My information about Rotary was obtained from the Internet. (www.rotary.org)

Dr. Jonas Salk and Dr. Albert Sabin made the world a better place with their vaccines. Many parents are grateful for their success.

Glossary

Arthrodesis: surgery to artificially induce joint ossification between bones

Arthroscopic surgery: pertaining to or giving correct vision

Astragal: the huckle bone or ankle bone; the upper bone of the foot

Bivalve: having to halves; splits into two parts, as the oyster

Formalin: a 40 percent solution of formaldehyde in water.

Poliomyelitis: inflammation of the spinal cord; an acute virus marked by fever, motor paralysis, and atrophy of skeletal muscles, often permanently disabling. Another name: infantile paralysis.

CPSIA information can be obtained at www.ICGtesting.com
Printed in the USA
LVOW041024040912

297275LV00002B/28/P